(UNANSWERED)
DISCUSSION GUIDE

 ANCHORSAWAY

Published by CrossSection
940 Calle Negocio #175
San Clemente, CA 92673
800-946-5983
crosssection.com

Scripture Taken from the Holy Bible, New International Version®, NIV®.
Copyright © 1973, 1978, 1984, 2011 by Biblica, Inc.™

Book + Jacket design by Crosssection
Set in Adobe Frutiger and Font Bureau Agency
First Edition: December 2014
Printed in the USA

ISBN 978-0-9899537-7-1

LESSON 1 | THE LAKE

We all have our own stories of suffering and disappointment. Nancy's story embraces the harsh reality of living in a broken world that is often far from what we expect and is beyond our understanding. It is how we cope with the suffering and disappointment that matters. Because of her age and lack of anyone speaking truth into her about the drowning incident and her role in it, she was left to her own reasoning in trying to deal with life on this planet.

Nancy chose to walk away from God because He scared her, and she feared that He would kill her. Over time, she concluded that she had no other choice but to live for herself and try her hardest to fill a huge void in her life.

Nancy had worked hard to find her identity—she played golf, earned degrees, got married, had children and gathered material possessions. But her efforts turned up short when she realized she felt no closer to finding her purpose or understanding life. She became convinced that there must be something or someone outside of herself that would provide peace, purpose and hope in this world. This led to her lifelong search to find out who God is and who she is. Sadly, she saw her Christian acquaintances as hypocrites. Others she tried to engage in conversations about Christianity did not fully understand their own beliefs, let alone how to share them. They were little help in leading her to a faith in Jesus.

If she had met you, would you have been someone in whom she could have found a reason to believe in God?

It is often said that Christians who are living out their faith may be the closest that some people ever get to reading the Bible, stepping into a church, or seeing a reflection of God's compassionate heart. We can do this by knowing God and loving others, so that they too might meet the One who can give them life to the full!

Scripture tells us that we are all created in the image of God, meaning we all have the opportunity to have a personal, eternal relationship with Him. When we do not understand how much God loves us and wants us to choose to love and trust Him, we might get the impression that God is distant. Nothing could be further from the truth. Even though we were born with a sin nature, which is the insatiable desire to do our own thing, we were also created with emptiness in our soul that can only be filled through a relationship with God.

Nancy experienced that void and realized that life without God does not work. The very things that she was trying to earn through performance, she found that God gives them freely when we believe in His Son. Things like love, joy, peace, patience, kindness, goodness, faithfulness, gentleness, self-control, purpose and understanding are all ours when we learn to trust in God.

> *"The Lord is not slow to fulfill his promise as some count slowness, but is patient toward you, not wishing that any should perish, but that all should reach repentance"* *(2 Peter 3:9).*

Once we believe in God and become His child, we are enabled through the Holy Spirit to love Him with all our heart, mind, soul and strength as we radically love others. He wants us to love Him by spending time getting to know Him. One of the best ways to do that is by reading Scripture and talking with Him (praying). Spending time with other Christians encourages us and gives us a better understanding of what it means to live out our faith in all areas of life. Some say that their faith is personal, so they are not interested in being with other Christians or talking with others about God. But God wants to use broken people like us to reflect His light to our family, friends, co-workers and complete strangers—often times without words! Nowhere in Scripture are any of us exempt from living out our faith and letting our light shine for all to see. If our faith is genuine, it will be evident to others.

Thankfully, Nancy's search did not stop with the Christians who weren't prepared to give an answer. Her answers came when she met people who loved her exactly as she was and were eager to encourage her. Many mentored her, explaining the deeper things of God, and as a result, she became a believer of Jesus, a student of the Scriptures, a teacher and writer of the Christian worldview. Now, her goal in life is to be used by God to help others know what they believe, how to give answers to those who are searching and how to reflect God's love and grace toward the people they meet along life's journey.

DISCUSSION QUESTIONS:

1. If Nancy had come to you and asked, "How do you know that Christianity is not a hoax?", would you have been able to give her a reasonable answer?

2. Have you ever had a time in your life where you questioned the goodness of God or even if there is a God during your time of suffering?

3. Why do you think that it is important to talk with others who have a strong faith in God as shown by the way they love others?

4. Would the people that you're around every day say that your life generally reflects Jesus?

5. Is there duplicity in the way you live and love?

LESSON 2 | THE SEARCH

In its proper place, performing can be a good thing, but when it drives our lives inside and outside of the church, it is exhausting and will ultimately result in burnout. Performance by definition means to fulfill an obligation or requirement, or to accomplish something as promised or expected. It always involves an audience—whether it is one person or many.[i]

Many of us, as well as our children, have become performance addicts. It makes sense when you think about it, because we start performance training early. We melt when a baby smiles at us and we applaud when a child takes her first step. Later, we cheer when he scores a goal and weep tears of joy when he receives a diploma. Our children who "behave" in the presence of friends by standing and shaking hands or who, on rare occasions, do the dishes, are celebrated. Then they go to school and are encouraged by peers to talk during class, sneak out of school early and go to a party with no parents present. They follow along! Later, in youth group, they sign up for a missionary trip in hopes of being put on the leadership team. Many of us will do almost anything to be liked, included and applauded. Long term, this approval-driven performance comes with a price tag. Before we know it, we know less about who we are as a person. And since popularity is temporary, we also have no peace and our lives feel out of control.

So what happens when we go into a church and begin to worship God, the Holy One? Most of us are familiar with Scripture verses that tell us that we become God's child by believing that Jesus died and rose again, making Him God our Savior (John 3:16, Romans 3:21-26, 1 Corinthians 15:1-5). No performance is required—He already loves all He has created. We hear this message of truth, but because we have been conditioned to perform in all other areas of our lives, many of us subconsciously feel we must do "God things" to secure His love and acceptance. We feel compelled to rarely, if ever, say "no" to anyone asking us to work at the church, teach a Bible study, or join committees. Our motivation is to please God rather than to trust Him. In the end, we become exhausted and wonder if this is what it means to have a relationship with God. We have reduced Him to just one more person for whom we are driven to perform, in the hope that He will love us more and show us mercy for all the good we have done and the bad things we have resisted.

> *"In sacrifice and offering you have not delighted, but you have given me an open ear. Burnt offering and sin offering you have not required...As for you, O LORD, you will not restrain your mercy from me; your steadfast love and your faithfulness will ever preserve me!...But may all who seek you rejoice and be glad in you; may those who love your salvation say continually, 'Great is the LORD'" (Psalm 40:6, 11, 16).*

Is it any wonder that more than half of all self-proclaiming Christians believe they can earn God's love and approval by performing for Him, that a "good" person who does good things can earn his or her salvation, and that there are many roads that lead to God? We haven't come to terms with the truth that God is not a better version of you or me—He is in a league of His own. Jesus was 100 percent human and 100 percent God. He is incapable of sinning, cannot lie and will never stop loving and pursuing us! How do we know? He clearly defines Himself in the Scriptures.

"God is not man, that he should lie, or a son of man, that he should change his mind. Has he said, and will he not do it? Or has he spoken, and will he not fulfill it?" (Numbers 23:19).

"Be strong and courageous. Do not fear or be in dread of them, for it is the LORD your God who goes with you. He will not leave you or forsake you" (Deuteronomy 31:6).

"For by grace you have been saved through faith. And this is not your own doing; it is the gift of God, not a result of works, so that no one may boast. For we are his workmanship, created in Christ Jesus for good works, which God prepared beforehand, that we should walk in them" (Ephesians 2:8-10).

DISCUSSION QUESTIONS:

1. Do you struggle with being trapped by trying to please God and do "good" things?

2. Can you know for sure that God loves and accepts you just as you are without trying to gain His approval through your own efforts?

3. Do you know anyone who loves you like God loves you? Is that possible?

4. Why might your friends, business associates or family members think that your love for them is based on their performance?

5. What does it mean to be "saved by grace"?

LESSON 3 | ALARMING REALITY

A war is being waged for the hearts and minds of God's family, young and old, and so far, we're not winning. Children, young adults and parents across the globe are walking away from their faith in God at a record pace. It should be no surprise—God has been pushed out of kindergarten, elementary and high schools. If our children don't walk away from Him before they leave home, up to 80 percent of them will by the time they graduate from college, with few returning. Colleges have become breeding grounds for atheism, and Christian students are easy prey if they are not prepared for the battle of defending their faith. The majority of secular professors will intimidate and shame Christian students early on in their college experience by telling them that belief in moral absolutes or in God makes them intolerant and judgmental. Even Christian professors are losing their jobs while others are not receiving well-earned promotions because of their belief in Jesus and the Bible. Sadly, this is happening in secular and Christian universities alike.

Maybe you have experienced this yourself or know someone who is struggling with his or her faith in Jesus. Many of the victims of our Godless culture are left wondering if there is a God and if so, what is He like? What does He think of us and what can we do to make Him love us? Others struggle with making time for God—with so much busyness in our lives, God is simply not on the top of our "must do" lists. As a result, confusion, unbelief and apathy reign in our personal lives, family, work and even within our churches.

Why this indifference toward Jesus? Many researchers think that it is because the Bible has been treated as a book of stories, and Sunday school and church have not been relevant to real life. Others say that questions about God and the Bible have not been encouraged or answered. Still some lament that the hows and whys of the Christian faith were never taught in church in a way that made sense so they lost interest in pursuing their faith. Yet, in the midst of such apathy, something inside all of us yearns to know God. There is an emptiness in this life that is not filled by the stuff we buy, the places we travel, the clothes we accumulate or the classes we take. Even getting married, having good friends, a job and children fail to satisfy the nagging need we have for fulfillment, purpose and contentment. Sadly, even among churchgoers who love God, few could engage in a conversation about how we know that the Bible is true and why God allows good people to suffer.

It is time to turn the tide, time to learn the foundations of the Christian faith and other belief systems so that we can better understand our family, friends and the people we have yet to meet. In this study, the goal is that you will not only see that the Christian faith is true and verifiable, but that it has the power to transform our lives.

Let's dive in. Take a few minutes to think about these questions that someone might ask you:

- Do all religions worship the same God? How do you know?

- How do you know that Christianity is not a hoax?

- What is a Christian? How do you know that you are one?

- Why are you a Christian?

- Would your co-workers know that you are a Christian by the way you work and interact with others?

- How do you know that Jesus is real?

- How do you know the Bible was written by God and is true and verifiable?

- What if you understood that the power God used to raise Jesus from the dead is available to you every day? What if you could live every day of your life, regardless of circumstances, with peace, joy, forgiveness and purpose because God himself, the Holy Spirit, lives in you? Would this change the way you think, love and live?

Can you answer these questions? We'll cover these and many more in this study. For more insight into the lessons and to dig deeper, read the *Unanswered: Smoke, Mirrors, and God* book as you work through the study guides.

DISCUSSION QUESTIONS:

1. What are your expectations of this study?

2. Why do you think so many people walk away from their faith? Are you one of them?

3. Do you have doubts about God that have caused you to question your own faith?

4. What are some questions that you have about your faith that you would like someone to answer?

5. If you do not understand something in the Bible, does that mean it is not true?

LESSON 4 | PERFORMANCE TRAP

Two guys were sitting in a room with glass walls. Both were snapping their fingers, bobbing their heads and tapping their feet in sync to the music. By observation, both were enjoying it. One was deaf. Which one was it?

Such it is with so many who are caught up in the performance predicament! We get so good at doing all the "right" Christian things that we not only fool others into thinking that we have a solid faith, but also we fool ourselves as well. In this case, imitation is not the greatest form of flattery. So many of us have been taught to "just have faith" with little or no substance behind it. God says that we should *"Love the Lord your God with all your heart and with all your soul and with all your mind and with all your strength" (Mark 12:30).* With a solid Christian worldview, through the work of the Holy Spirit abiding in us, we will be thoroughly equipped to live out Christ in all of life, instead of just doing good works to prove to someone, maybe even ourselves, that we're a Christian.

The heartbeat of the Christian worldview is a firm understanding of the fundamental truths of the Christian faith. Becoming a Christian means to believe that Jesus is our Savior. *"For God so loved the world, that he gave his only begotten Son, that whoever believes in him should not perish, but have everlasting life" (John 3:16).* Note here that belief is an action, not a passive idea. This action includes knowing who God says He is and who He says we are. The Christian worldview is an understanding that the Bible is God's way of speaking truth to us as we read and pray through its pages. It is learning how to defend the Bible and how to defend Jesus so that when people ask questions, we will be able to give the reason for the hope that we have in God. It goes way beyond performing; it is a life well lived with and through Christ in all we do. The desire for human approval turns to trusting our Lord to guide us personally in all areas of life. The best part of all of this is that with Christ living in us, we will experience all that we have ever wanted: total acceptance, love, hope, security, forgiveness and the desire to love God and others well. It is the death of the great divide between Christ and other areas of our lives—He is invited into every moment of every day.

Everyone has a worldview. Simply defined, a worldview is the foundation from which one thinks, acts, looks at life, and responds to the world in which he or she lives. To better understand worldviews, we are going to ask basic life questions of the Christian, Humanist and Postmodernist worldviews and compare their answers to one another. These questions are: From where did I come? Why is the world such a mess? Is there any hope? What is my purpose in life? What happens when I die?

The Christian worldview responses to these questions are:

1. From where did I come?

"In the beginning God created the heavens and the earth" (Genesis 1:1).

The universe and everything in it was created by the Personal, Creator God. All people were created in God's image to bring God glory!

2. Why is the world such a mess?

"All have sinned and fallen short of the glory of God" (Romans 3:23).

The first man and the first woman chose to rebel against God, changing the beauty and order of things on this earth forever. Fellowship with God was broken and could only be restored by Jesus' death on the cross for the sins of all people.

3. Is there any hope?

Our hope is not in the smoke, mirrors, friends or in our Christian work. It is in Christ and Christ alone.

"We have this as a sure and steadfast anchor of the soul, a hope that enters into the inner place behind the curtain" (Hebrews 6:19).

4. What is my purpose in life?

Our purpose on earth is to love God, to love others and to live life to the fullest (Matthew 22:36-40; John 10:10)!

5. What happens when I die?

Those who believe in Jesus Christ, the Messiah, will live forever with Him in heaven (John 3:16, 14:2-3; Revelation 21:1-4).

It seems so simple, and it is, profoundly so. Living out the Christian life is the most exciting journey anyone could ever experience. After looking at each worldview's answers, the big question is: Which worldviews lead to life and which ones lead to death? The Christian worldview, with Christ at the center, leads to life!

DISCUSSION QUESTIONS:

1. What's a worldview?

2. How would you describe the Christian worldview?
   Does performance have anything to do with it?

3. Do most Christians live out the Christian worldview?
   Why or why not?

4. Is the life of a Christian easy?
   What makes it so difficult at times?

5. If you were on trial for being a Christian who loves God and
   others, would you be found guilty?

LESSON 5 | FIGHT CLUB

The essence of Postmodernism can be found by reading a few lines from the script of "Fight Club." In it, Brad Pitt plays Tyler Durden. The members of the Fight Club are gathered together and Tyler addresses the group, "Man, I see in fight club the strongest and smartest men who've ever lived. I see all this potential, and I see squandering...an entire generation pumping gas, waiting tables; slaves with white collars. Advertising has us chasing cars and clothes, working jobs we hate so we can buy stuff we don't need. We're the middle children of history, man. No purpose or place. We have no Great War. No Great Depression. Our Great War's a spiritual war... our Great Depression is our lives. We've all been raised on television to believe that one day we'd all be millionaires, and movie gods, and rock stars. But we won't."

Postmodernism is not driven by truth, or by scientific absolutes, but by the culture. People who embrace this worldview ignore God, His saving grace and His authority. They turn instead to a symphony of conflicting philosophies that, in its purest form, leads to lives without hope. As a result, today's Postmodernists are the most depressed generation to have ever lived with the highest number of suicides ever recorded. The key word for the Postmodernist is, "whatever." It can be used as the answer for any question that you might ask. For a worldview that is all about feeling good, they have sadly missed the mark.

Postmodernists pride themselves on being tolerant toward all people, no matter what others believe, except of course with Christians. When Christians refuse to accept their ideas as being equally true and valid as their own, the Postmodernists are quick to brand Christ followers as intolerant and judgmental. This extreme relativism is particularly prevalent on the college campuses and in the workplace. It is through this high-pressured intimidation that many Christians are rendered defenseless because they simply have not built their faith on a rock solid foundation that can counter such tactics. Is it any wonder that so many Christians are walking away from their faith?

To read the works of Postmodernists, you might well drive yourself nuts. Look at the following quotes from this worldview (that according to them, is not a worldview at all).

"There are no hard distinctions between what is real and what is unreal, nor between what is true and what is false. A thing is not necessarily either true or false; it can be both true and false." —Harold Pinter [2]

"We're the most aggressively inarticulate generation to come along since, you know, a long time ago!" —Taylor Mal [3]

"Amusing and perfectly self-conscious charlatans." —Noam Chomsky [4]

Christian author David Wells notes, "In our postmodern culture which is TV dominated, image sensitive, and morally vacuous, personality is everything and character is increasingly irrelevant." [5]

How would Postmodernism answer the 5 life questions?

1. **From where did I come?**

    We are the result of random, impersonal, undirected forces of nature. Others have their opinions.

2. **Why is there such a mess in the world?**

    People who advocate universal truths, like Christians, create havoc in this world.

3. **Is there any hope?**

    No.

4. **What is my purpose in life?**

    Whatever.

5. **What happens when I die?**

    Whatever.

As we examine these answers, one can see that the Postmodern worldview does not lead to life, but rather to a spiritual and emotional death. Again, it is good to remind ourselves that God loves and continues to pursue those who have not yet put their trust in Him. Postmoderns are looking in all the wrong places for what only God can give them.

DISCUSSION QUESTIONS:

1. How does Postmodernism differ from Christianity?

2. What do you think is the reason for the depression this worldview encompasses?

3. How might you "speak" into this worldview without using words?

4. How can you encourage young people who are preparing to go to college?

5. How might some Christians fall into the Postmodern way of thinking?

LESSON 6 | OH MY GOD

It is no secret that the world is a mess. Nightly news programs are filled with stories of how appalling the world around us has become. We hear of famine, human trafficking, cancer and devastating natural disasters. Shootings in schoolyards, families in crisis, depression and suicides are at an all-time high. As human beings, when we see and experience some of these terrifying things, we often become angry with God and begin to question His love, goodness and faithfulness. How could a good, loving, all-knowing, all-powerful God allow suffering to happen to any created person, let alone to His own children? Is this punishment for something we have done? Why us?

As we search for answers to suffering, it is comforting to know that Christianity embraces suffering. We are saved because Jesus Christ suffered and died for us all, paying the price for your sin and mine. There was purpose in His suffering. He did not deserve it, but because He loved us in such an incredibly awesome and mysterious way, He willingly died so that we might have life. From the beginning of time, since Adam and Eve's first rebellion in the Garden of Eden, men and women have desired to go their own way, away from God. This rebellion is sin, that is at the root of all things that cause us pain.

As a result of that first sin, we, as humans, are sinners both by nature and by choice. We live in a broken world that is filled with broken people. We can read a newspaper or watch television to see that mankind is very capable of doing evil things to one another, things that bring about much suffering. C.S. Lewis, author of The Problem of Pain, estimates that 80 percent of all pain is caused by human agents.[6] We do great damage to one another: physically, mentally, emotionally and spiritually. I think that we all can agree that by nature, we are incredibly selfish and want things to go our own way. One person's sin can cause many of us to suffer, sometimes in ways we never fully recover. This is no surprise to God, but He offers this encouragement for all of us who suffer:

> "I have told you these things, so that in me you may have peace. In this world you will have trouble. But take heart! I have overcome the world" (John 16:33).

C.S. Lewis said:

> "Pain insists upon being attended to. God whispers to us in our pleasures, speaks in our conscience and shouts in our pain. It is His megaphone to rouse a deaf world." [7]

There is purpose in everything God does and does not do. When God allows us to suffer, it is for a purpose. Perhaps it is to pull us back into a stronger dependence on Him—to know that without Him, we are without hope. It is often in the midst of the deepest valleys that we are closest to God and His comfort, love and peace. With prayer, love and tenderness, it is a time for Christians to step up and be the hands and feet of Jesus as they pour into those who suffer. From God's perspective, suffering is very much a part of this life and, as strange as it may seem, we are called to expect it, embrace it and grow closer to God through it.

"Consider it pure joy, my brothers and sisters whenever you face trials of many kinds, because you know that the testing of your faith produces perseverance. Let perseverance finish its work so that you may be mature and complete, not lacking anything. If any of you lacks wisdom, you should ask God, who gives generously to all without finding fault, and it will be given to you" (James 1:2-5).

It is through suffering that most of us realize that we cannot simply "fix it" ourselves—we need some big time help to get us through. As we go to God in moments like this, He hears us and is glad that we have come to Him. He does not desire for us to hurt or suffer; He does not desire for us to be in pain for pain's sake. What He does desire is for us to know the all-surpassing greatness of His love no matter what we are facing. That is what allows each of us to live life to the fullest!

"The thief comes only to steal and kill and destroy. I came that they may have life and have it abundantly. I am the good shepherd. The good shepherd lays down his life for the sheep" (John10:10-11).

"I am the vine; you are the branches. Whoever abides in me and I in him, he it is that bears much fruit, for apart from me you can do nothing" (John 15:5).

What would it be like if God's children learned to suffer well? What if in our own suffering, we were a light to others? What if we were the first to forgive or the first to ask for forgiveness from someone? What would happen if we knew that God is sovereign, that our suffering had purpose? What if we looked for ways to bring honor and glory to God through our own pain?

"On the last day of the feast, the great day, Jesus stood up and cried out, 'If anyone thirsts, let him come to me and drink. Whoever believes in me, as the Scripture has said, 'Out of his heart will flow rivers of living water'" (John 7:37-38).

In our times of suffering, it is important to be honest with God. He already knows our innermost thoughts and words before we speak them. As only a perfect, loving Father can do, He may not answer all of our "whys," but He will provide comfort, peace, joy, strength and patience in any situation. He is here with us today and every day. He will never leave us—ever.

DISCUSSION QUESTIONS:

1. Why is there so much suffering in the world?

2. How does the presence of suffering affect your relationship with Jesus Christ?

3. Is suffering always bad?

4. Would you be more or less effective in comforting others who struggle with pain and suffering if you had suffered yourself?

5. Discuss ways that others have ministered to you in a way that provided comfort and encouragement when you were suffering.

LESSON 7 | I AM

Is there a way to learn who God truly is, or is He merely defined by someone's opinion? When our image of God is based only on past experiences or on what others have said, we have no way of being sure of whom He is. What then is our standard of truth?

Ask the man or woman on the street and you will get answers that range from one end of the spectrum to the other. "He is good and loving" to "He is vengeful and full of anger." Others say, "He doesn't exist," or "I don't know if He exists." The Pantheists would say that God is in everything and in everybody. The list of responses is endless. All of these cannot be true. Is there a God? If so, is it possible to know Him?

The Triunity of God

God wasted no time defining who He is in Genesis 1:1: *"In the beginning God created."* The Hebrew word for God is "Elohim," a singular masculine noun that is plural in nature. Verse 26 says, *"Then God said, "Let us make man in our image, after our likeness."* Many scholars believe that this is the reflection of the Trinity.

The significance of the Trinity for us can be better understood when we look at this truth: One of the foundational beliefs of Christianity, which sets it apart from all other religious cults and belief systems, is the conviction that Jesus is truly God. In no way does Jesus play a supporting role to the Father and the Holy Spirit. He is fully God just as they are, an equal member of the Trinity. If someone says to you, "I believe in God, but not Jesus," you would know immediately that the person with whom you are speaking is, at best, confused. God is not God without Jesus. God is not God without the Father. And God is not God without the Holy Spirit. God is one being with three persons.

The Holy Spirit

> *"You, however, are controlled not by the sinful nature but by the Spirit, if the Spirit of God lives in you. And if anyone does not have the Spirit of Christ, he does not belong to Christ"* (Romans 8:9).

Because Christ paid the penalty for our sin, we have a restored relationship with God. He wants to be in a personal relationship with each of us on a moment-by-moment basis, which is why He has given us the Holy Spirit. Imagine, God living in you! Under the Old Covenant, the Holy Spirit was sent to be with those whom the Father had chosen. Now in the New Covenant, the Holy Spirit lives in, or indwells, the believer. Upon belief, God sends the Holy Spirit, the Comforter, to dwell in the believer and be a guide for living out their faith in every area of life. No doubt, this is a lifelong process!

To find out who God is, we must listen to how He defines Himself. The Word of God, the Bible, is full of His attributes. One of the encouraging things about God is that He is who He says He is all the time. He cannot be loving and unfaithful. He cannot be all-powerful and unrighteous. Even though we often don't understand or can't make sense of much that happens in this world, God does. Unlike us, God's character is unchanging. "Every good and perfect gift is from above, coming down from the Father of the heavenly lights, who does not change like shifting shadows" (James 1:17).

The Attributes of God through the Scriptures

1. **The One True God.** There is only one God and He is the God of the Scriptures.

   "I am the LORD, and there is no other; apart from me there is no God. I will strengthen you, though you have not acknowledged me, so that from the rising of the sun to the place of its setting men may know there is none besides me. I am the LORD and there is no other" (Isaiah 45:5-6).

2. **All Knowing.** He knows everything that has happened, is occurring right now and will happen in the future. There is nothing that God does not know.

   "You know when I sit and when I rise; you perceive my thoughts from afar. You discern my going out and my lying down; you are familiar with all my ways. Before a word is on my tongue, you know it completely, O LORD" (Psalm139:2-4).

3. **All Powerful.** He is not limited by anything. He alone possesses all power.

   "But Jesus looked at them and said, 'With man this is impossible, but with God all things are possible'" (Matthew 19:26).

4. **Faithful.** God can always be depended on to do what He says and He will fulfill His promises.

   "If we are faithless, he remains faithful—for he cannot deny himself" (2 Timothy 2:13).

5. **Personal.** God interacts with us personally and we can respond to Him as persons.

   "Keep your life free from love of money, and be content with what you have, for he has said, 'I will never leave you nor forsake you'" (Hebrews 13:5).

6. **Righteous (Just).** God always does what is right, for He alone is the absolute standard of right and wrong.

"The Rock, his work is perfect, for all his ways are justice. A God of faithfulness and without iniquity, just and upright is he" (Deuteronomy 32:4).

7. **Love.** He loves unconditionally always for our benefit. He finds pleasure in us, His creation and always wants what is best for us.

"For I am convinced that neither death nor life, neither angels nor demons, neither the present nor the future, nor any powers, neither height nor depth, nor anything else in all creation, will be able to separate us from the love of God that is in Christ Jesus our Lord" (Romans 8:38-39).

If, or when, we truly embrace the God of the Scriptures, He will totally change our lives. We are loved just as we are by the Creator of the Universe. We are fully forgiven, loved no matter what, never lied to or deceived, and never left alone. We can trust Him completely and even call Him our friend. There is no greater joy.

DISCUSSION QUESTIONS:

1. How would you best describe the Triunity of God?

2. How is God's love different from human love?

3. Would knowing who God truly is change the way you approach suffering?

4. God always reflects all of his attributes. How might that change the way you see Him?

5. How can a true understanding of God help you begin to find peace about some difficult things in your life?

LESSON 8 | I DOUBT IT

If God is who He says He is, if salvation through His Son is open to all who believe and if the paper trail verifying the authenticity of the Scriptures is unending, why then are we so easily tossed and turned in the waves of doubt? Why is it so hard, seemingly impossible, to maintain a strong faith in the midst of the chaos of our lives? Salvation for our sins comes from belief and not works. We understand that, but still we question. We feel at times that there is a war raging in our minds and hearts as we continually fight the desire to live for ourselves instead of living in and for Christ.

The origin of darkness and doubt can be traced to Genesis 3:1-5 when Satan tempted Eve by saying, *"Did God really say, 'You must not eat from any tree in the garden?'" (Genesis 3:1).* The first of many lies from Satan's mouth was a question intended to cause doubt. Up to this point, neither Adam nor Eve had entertained doubt. But, under the pressure of Satan's temptation, they both entertained the notion of uncertainty, which led to the idea that God was withholding pleasure from them. They bit, and the rest is history. Still, to this day, Satan continues to wreak havoc in the hearts and minds of many Christians who not only are skeptical of the nature of God, but also are convinced that God does not want them to enjoy life. Often, it is not until we taste the consequences of our doubt that we realize Satan is a liar and that God is truth and wants the very best for us, always!

Addressing doubt and questions can be overwhelming and complex because emotions often take over. Effectively dealing with unbelief is a process. To be able to claim understanding and victory over most of our doubt takes perseverance and hard work. Those who are willing to allow God to unravel their misconceptions about life, and others including God often become strong and confident in their faith.

Stubborn Doubt

One kind of doubt is stubborn. It is the kind of disbelief that says, "No matter what you say, no matter what evidence says, I choose not to believe in God in any way, shape or form." Sir Fred Hoyle, an English astronomer from Cambridge University, said, "The chance that higher life forms might have emerged in this way (evolution) is comparable with the chance that 'a tornado sweeping through a junkyard might assemble a Boeing 747 from the materials therein."[8] Hoyle chose to reject truth and believed the lie that life had been formed through evolution.

Reasonable Doubt

God loves it when people who have doubts and questions are not afraid to face them and work through them until they get an answer. These people are seekers that simply want to know more, but do not know where to go for answers. They might doubt the resurrection of Jesus because it makes no sense. Often times, doubts of the mind can be satisfied by studying the Word of God, reading reliable outside resources, and talking with men and women who have godly wisdom.

Heartfelt Doubt

There are also doubts of the heart and emotions that cannot be satisfied through reading and studying. These doubts come from those who are suffering deeply. Only God Himself can quiet a broken heart. No matter who you are, or what you have done or gone through, God is there with you and for you. He hears your prayers and often times may weep with you. He wants you to know Him, to learn from Him and to talk to Him. You matter a great deal to God. He died for you, not only to offer you forgiveness for your sins and eternal life, but also so that He might have a relationship with you that is real, life giving, and full of hope, joy, and peace.

Whether you are struggling with stubborn, reasonable or heartfelt doubt, God wants to meet you right where you are! He promises that if you look for Him, you will find Him. Where should you look? Your answers will be found in the Scriptures, in prayer and through friends who are wise and are living out their faith. Remember that God is faithful and wants you to have true peace and joy. If you seek, you will find. No doubt about it!

DISCUSSION QUESTIONS

1. From where did doubt come?

2. What is stubborn doubt and why is it potentially so hurtful?

3. Are there answers for someone with reasonable doubt?

4. What is the good news for someone who has heartfelt doubt?

5. Can any good come from doubt?

LESSON 9 | THE "I" OF THE STORM

A Christian and a Humanist are both paleontologists who are examining layers of rock filled with animal and plant imprints. As they uncover the fossils preserved in the rocks, the scientist who is a Christian is struck by the beauty and intricacy of God's creation in each of his findings. He sees the smaller fossilized fish and insects as unique and distinctly different created things. He sees the strata in the rock formations and is reminded of the worldwide flood written in Genesis.

"The flood continued forty days on the earth. The waters increased and bore up the ark, and it rose high above the earth. The waters prevailed and increased greatly on the earth, and the ark floated on the face of the waters. And the waters prevailed so mightily on the earth that all the high mountains under the whole heaven were covered. The waters prevailed above the mountains, covering them fifteen cubits deep" (Genesis 7:17-20).

Next to the Christian scientist, the Humanist scientist sees the plants and animals as a result of chance and evolution in action. He sees the bug as an animal that, over millions of years, would evolve into higher life forms. Because the Humanist rejects the idea of a Creator God, he has no choice but to believe that the plants and animals and even human beings evolve by chance over time, even though there is no scientific explanation for such events. From goo to you by random selection is the Humanist explanation for the existence all things.

The following are quotes from noted evolutionists:

"The absence of fossil evidence for intermediary stages between major transitions in organic design, indeed our inability, even in our imagination, to construct functional intermediates in many cases, has been a persistent and nagging problem for gradualist accounts of evolution." Stephen Jay Gould (Professor of Geology and Paleontology, Harvard University)[9]

"Echoing the criticism made of his father's habilis skulls, he added that Lucy's skull was so incomplete that most of it was 'imagination made of plaster of Paris,' thus making it impossible to draw any firm conclusion about what species she belonged to." Referring to comments made by Richard Leakey (Director of National Museums of Kenya)[10]

Though the Humanism/Naturalism worldview largely emerged in Europe during the Renaissance, we can trace its origin back to the Garden of Eden where Satan successfully tempted Adam and Eve to become focused on themselves instead of on trusting God. This European movement deeply impacted the educational system by focusing on man's reason as the answer for all the problems that men and women wrestled with during the 17th and 18th centuries. Charles Darwin, active in the mid-1800s, provided an excuse for many to abandon their faith in God. In the name of flawed science, he laid the foundation for the atheistic scientist to explain away the Creator God by ushering in the theory of natural selection. By the 1930s, Humanism made its way to the United States, one nation under God, and by the 60s and 70s people were walking away from their faith and church in droves.

It is frightening what happens to a culture when men and women reject God and choose to live a me-centered existence. Without God there is no purpose in life because, if we believe what the Humanist tells us, we are the result of random chance and luck. With no God, there are no moral absolutes, so anything goes. Why not? Who will judge? Without God, there is chaos. Without God, there is also no forgiveness and therefore no hope to spend eternity with Him in heaven where love, joy and peace rule. Imagine—none of this will be available to the Humanist solely because they refuse to believe in God.

Most all of us struggle to some degree with the drive (some would call it a compulsion) to perform. The humanistic worldview has conditioned us to believe that our self-image is totally dependent on our performance. Accumulating wealth, reaching a status that others look up to or lust after, and being liked and admired by others is the prime focus of the heart of a Humanist. This worldview is not about being a servant: sacrificially giving and wanting no credit for what was done—instead, it is all about ME. This is why performance not only dominates the workplace, but can also be a leading force in the church. Furthermore, the influx of Humanism in our culture has affected us all emotionally, mentally and physically. According to many physicians, out of control busyness is directly related to increased anxiety, heart attacks and many other illnesses.

How then, would the Humanist answer the life questions?

1. From where did I come? The universe evolved over millions of years. It is the result of random impersonal, undirected forces of nature. In the beginning was the Big Bang. God had nothing to do with it because there is no God.

2. Why is there such a mess in the world? Man is good, but has not been self-actualized. Until people can become more perfect, they will struggle. Religion and a belief in God are the source of the evil in the world.

3. Is there any hope? Man is the savior of people. Utopia is possible.

4. What is my purpose in life? To become smarter, do more, earn more money, be a winner in sports and at work, and be someone that everyone else wants to be like.

5. What happens when I die? Life ends. I go into the ground and become dirt.

Hopefully, those who live out the Humanist worldview will begin to question the value of living a performance-based existence that is reminiscent of a hamster on the run. It ultimately takes them nowhere. Sadly, unlike the Christian worldview, the Humanist worldview ends in a spiritual, mental and emotional death. The good news is that even as these individuals live through such a godless worldview, God still loves and pursues them. Perhaps He is counting on you to be that light that may cause a friend or co-worker to begin to question their journey, especially as they see Jesus in you by the way you love them and accept them just as they are!

DISCUSSION QUESTIONS:

1. How would you describe a Humanist? Is there hope for them to find God?

2. What do Humanism and Christianity have in common? How do they differ?

3. What are your options for knowing where you and other life came from if you do not believe in God?

4. Have you adopted any of the tenants of the Humanist worldview without realizing it?

5. With love and respect, how can you best challenge a Humanist to re-think his worldview?

LESSON 10 | A LOVE LETTER

Many people embrace the flawed notion that absolute truth does not exist. In doing so, they have chosen to navigate life without a moral compass and are left drifting, *"tossed to and fro by the waves and carried about by every wind of doctrine" (Ephesians 4:14)*. In the next few lessons, we are going to answer the questions: "Is the Bible authentic and is it historically reliable?" and "Could man have written the Bible without God?"

Knowing for sure that the Bible is the Word of God is a critical component in building a Christian worldview. In the Christian faith, the Bible is the foundation for all that we believe to be true about God, the Holy Spirit and the person of Jesus Christ. There is one continuous theme throughout all of Scripture: The redemption of man. It's not a story of man's search for God, but rather a message of God's desire to pursue and reveal Himself to man.

If the Bible is not true and not distinctly different from all other religious books, then we might rightly conclude that all roads lead to God. Most Christians however, will agree that the Bible is the Word of God, but few can explain why. How do we know that the Bible, and therefore Christianity are nothing more than a figment of someone's imagination, a big lie, that has been perpetuated for thousands of years? Can we prove, beyond a reasonable doubt, that the Bible is true? Is it more than just a collection of books written by men? Could man have written it without God?

Biblical historians say that the Bible is unique from any other book of antiquity. It contains 66 books written by 40 different authors, on 3 continents, through 3 languages (Hebrew, Greek and Aramaic), over 1,500 years. Many of the authors had drastically different backgrounds, including a poor fisherman, prime minister, king, herdsmen, tax collector, a doctor and a former murderer of Christians. The writers were diverse in age, education, personality, profession and circumstance, showing that God uses ordinary people to do amazing things with and for Him. In spite of that diversity, all of the books were written in harmony with the others, but with no collaboration among authors except for the Spirit of God speaking through them. The Jews looked at the Bible as God's love letter to His people.

To examine the authenticity of the Bible, we need to learn how the manuscripts were passed down through time. What was it about the way the scribes copied the material that would show that the process was done meticulously and with fidelity? The following overview will show how the Bible passed this test with flying colors.

The scribes, whose name means counter, were Jews, chosen by God to ensure the reliability of the documents. They meticulously copied these manuscripts letter by letter, counted the number of times each letter of the alphabet occurred in each book, and calculated the middle word of each book. If more than three mistakes existed in the manuscript, it was destroyed. This, in itself, sets the Bible apart from all other religious books.

"All scripture is God-breathed and is useful for teaching, rebuking, correcting and training in righteousness, so that the man of God may be thoroughly equipped for every good work" (2 Timothy 3:16-17).

How does the New Testament compare to other widely accepted books of antiquity that were penned by authors such as Plato and Homer? Plato's writings were written between 427-347 BC, with the earliest copy found dating from 900 AD. This means that the time span between the original manuscript and the most recent copy we have is 1,200 years. The shorter the time span, the greater the accuracy of the document. Another point to note is that there are only seven copies of Plato's writings surviving since that time. The greater the number of copies, the more accurate the writings. Students of philosophy rarely, if ever, question the reliability of Plato's words. Homer's Iliad is a more reliable book because it was written in 900 BC, with the earliest copy dating from 400 BC. That means the time span between the original manuscript and the most recent copy is only 500 years, and 643 copies of the book have survived. So, how does the New Testament compare to these widely read and accepted books of antiquity? The New Testament was written between 40-100 AD with the earliest copy dating from AD 125, which is only 25 years from the original manuscript with an astounding 24,000 copies that have survived!

Writer and historian Floyd McElveen wrote in his book, God's Word, Final, Infallible and Forever, "Even if someone deliberately or by accident amended or corrupted a manuscript, it would be corrected by the many other manuscripts available. To sum up: unless we want to throw a blanket over all of history and say that there is nothing knowable about the past, no history that can be trusted, no Grecian or Roman history, no Aristotle or Plato or Socrates, we had better not make any claims against the historicity and accuracy of the New Testament. The New Testament documents are far more numerous, older, demonstrably more accurate historically, and have been examined by a far greater battery of scholars, both friend and foe, than all the other ancient manuscripts put together. They have met the test impeccably!"[11]

The extensive research that has been done to prove and to disprove the reliability of the New Testament leaves the most ardent skeptic to agree that, when looking at the way the New Testament was written and passed down through time, it stands alone from all other books of antiquity. Only God could have breathed into such a book. In Science and Numbers, we will learn about the uniqueness of the Bible with its prophecies, archeological support and the writings from historians in the time of the early Church.

DISCUSSION QUESTIONS:

1. What would you say to someone who says that the Bible is nothing more than random make-believe stories written for weak-minded people?

2. Does it take more faith to believe the Bible is the truth inspired by God or to NOT believe in its reliability?

3. Why did God give us the Bible?

4. Could man have written the Bible without God?

5. Of all the reasons proving the reliability of the Bible, which was most meaningful to you?

LESSON 11 | SCIENCE + NUMBERS

The greatest claim of the God of the Bible is found in Isaiah 44:6 *"I am the first, and I am the last; and besides me there is no other God."* This all-powerful, all-knowing, unchanging, Creator God also foretold events of human history, left His thumbprint on archaeological findings and provided historical writers more than enough information to record events of the life of Jesus. In this lesson, we are going to look at the internal evidence that will add greater understanding and proof of the Bible's reliability.

The Bible is the only religious book of antiquity that contains prophecy in both the Old and New Testaments. The Bible contains more than 2,000 prophecies, with over 300 specifically about Jesus, the Messiah. When taking out the overlapping prophecies about the coming Savior, we are left with 48 pure, stand-alone prophecies. If just one of these prophecies does not come true, then Jesus of Nazareth is not the Messiah, and the Bible is not to be trusted. Furthermore, Christianity must then be regarded as a false religion. As you will see, such is not the case.

The question we are asking is, "What are the odds of one man fulfilling all 48 prophecies about the coming Messiah?" Some examples of fulfilled prophecy include Jesus being born in Bethlehem (Micah 5:2 and fulfilled in Matthew 2:1), preceded by a messenger, John the Baptist (Isaiah 40:3 and fulfilled in John 1:23), Jesus entering Jerusalem on a donkey (Zechariah 9:9 and fulfilled in Matthew 21:6-11) and Jesus' pierced hands and feet (Psalm 22:16, Isaiah 53:5 and fulfilled in Luke 23:33).

In his book, Science Speaks, Peter Stoner points out that if there were only eight prophecies about Jesus, the probability of one man fulfilling all of them would be 10^{17}. In order to better understand these odds, think of the state of Texas covered two feet deep in silver dollars with just one coin marked. Send out a blindfolded man and have him pick up the marked coin in his first try. The probability of that coin being the one that is marked is 10^{17}. With the fulfillment of 16 prophecies, the probability number would be 10^{45}. That number can better be represented by imagining a ball of silver dollars whose radius is 30 times the distance from the earth to the sun. Again, mark one coin in that ball and send in a blindfolded man to choose one. For one man to fulfill all 48 prophecies, the probability is 1 in 10^{150}. There is no concept model for this number. Jesus fulfilled all 48 prophecies perfectly. Conclusion: Jesus is the Messiah, the Son of the living God![12]

Since the Bible is a religious book, many take the position that it cannot be trusted unless we have corroborating evidence from extra-biblical sources. Archaeological discoveries are widespread and have greatly added to the reliability of the Scriptures. One of the greatest findings was the discovery of the

Dead Sea Scrolls. These scrolls were discovered in 1947 by a Bedouin shepherd boy who threw a rock in a cave along the northwest side of the Dead Sea. He heard something break, climbed into the cave and found large pottery jars that contained the greatest manuscript discovery of modern times. These manuscripts were copies of sections of every Old Testament book except Esther. These scrolls gave us the Hebrew text that was written 1,000 years earlier than the older manuscript copies. Many scholars analyzed the older and newer manuscripts to see how they matched up with each other. It was incredible! Save for about 13 punctuation and spelling variations, they matched!

What about evidence for the reliability of the Bible from outside sources who were not followers of Jesus? Once again, God has provided such proof in brilliant detail. Among them were Tacitus, Josephus, Suetonius, Eusebius of Caesarea and Pliny the Younger. Probably the best-known writer of Jesus' era was Flavius Josephus (37-100 AD), a Jewish historian who wrote one of the most comprehensive histories of the Jewish people for the non-Jewish world. In The Antiquities of the Jews, 18.3.3, he wrote: "Now there was about this time Jesus, a wise man, (if it be lawful to call him a man,) for he was a doer of wonderful works, a teacher of such men as receive the truth with pleasure. He drew over to him both many of the Jews, and many of the Gentiles. (He was the Christ) and when Pilate, at the suggestion of the principal men amongst us, had condemned him to the cross, those that loved him at the first did not forsake him, (for he appeared to them alive again the third day) as the divine prophets had foretold these and ten thousand other wonderful things concerning him; and the tribe of Christians, so named from him, are not extinct to this day."[13]

Yes, the Bible is an amazing collection of books written by men who were inspired by God. We know that it is unique in the way it was written and in how it compares to other religious books. It also separates itself from all other religious books in the foretelling of events. The multitude of archeological findings that support the Bible's writings, along with the vast support of writers from that day who wrote what they had seen and heard about Jesus, stand up to anyone who dares to challenge its reliability.

DISCUSSION QUESTIONS:

1. If Jesus were to ask you, "Who do you say I am?", what would be your response?

2. Which person of the Trinity do all cults and false religions misrepresent?

3. Do you know people of different faiths? Would they see you as a light for Christ by the way you live and love them?

4. Why do you think the world pushes people to accept all religions as equally valid?

5. What does it mean that all religions other than Christianity believe in a system of salvation based on good works?

LESSON 12 | NOT WHAT I EXPECTED

Who helped you form your understanding of God (or of no God)? Be it good or bad, most of us initially tend to form our understanding of who God is by what our parents have taught us and how they have lived out their faith. This is one of the reasons why discussions about God can be so emotional. The Christian mother teaches her son about God, as does the Hindu mother and the Mormon mom about their god. All are sincere and all think they are speaking truth to their child. The question is: Are all moms teaching their children the truth about God?

As we grow older, most often our faith changes to reflect our experiences with family, friends, church, movies, life crises and even misbehaving people of faith. By the time we reach our late teens, we will likely be completely confused about who we are and who God is. The result is that most people will walk away from their faith frustrated while others will make up their own rules for a belief system that works for them. Yet, in the midst of this broken world that we live in, some will trust God and be the light that Jesus teaches us to be by the way we live and communicate love to others.

Is there absolute Truth? Is there a way to find it? Do all religions worship the same God? How do different religions perceive Jesus? A simple, unbiased comparative analysis of different religions will give us some of the answers.

Hindus who subscribe to Philosophical Hinduism believe that God is an "it," and in Popular Hinduism, there are great multitudes of gods, including man. Hindus give no recognition of any kind to Christ. Similarly, most Buddhist sects are polytheistic, pantheistic or atheistic and give no recognition to Christ. Islam is the religion of the Muslims. They believe that there is only one god named Allah, who cannot be the same as the God of the Bible because his character and attributes differ from the God of the Scriptures. Furthermore, they see Jesus Christ as nothing more than a prophet of Allah.

Jesus asked the question:

"Who do people say that I am?" (Mark 8:27).

Contrary to the politically correct police, no two religions define God and Jesus Christ the same way; therefore, not all religions are the same. This leaves us to conclude that either they are all false religions, meaning that no religion is verifiable, or that one religion embraces truth and can be proven. Is there a religion that is both transformational and verifiable? The answer is, "Yes!"

Christianity is unique from other religions in many ways. Most notably, Jesus is the cornerstone of the Christian religion. All other religions, including cults, deny the deity of Christ. God never left open the option of believing that Jesus is a god, a good person or a prophet. Plain and simple, Jesus is God. In Christianity, the Bible is consistent in its portrayal of Christ's deity. This may surprise you, but Jesus is called:

- **Creator** (John 1:3, Colossians 1:15-17, Hebrews 1:10)

- **Lord of Lords and King of Kings** (Revelation 17:14, 19:16, 1 Timothy 6:14-16)

- **Savior** (Acts 2:21, 4:12, Romans 10:9)

- **Rock** (1 Corinthians 10:4, Isaiah 8:14)

- **The First and the Last** (Revelation 1:17, 2:8, 22:13)

- **Judge** (2 Timothy 4:1, 2 Corinthians 5:10, Romans 14:10)

- **I AM** (John 8:24, 58, 13:19, 18:5)

Christianity is the only religion that embraces the belief that a person becomes a child of God the moment he or she believes that Jesus Christ died on a cross and rose again to pay the penalty for his or her sins. Becoming a Christian is a gift of God's grace extended to all people on earth. In Christianity, salvation does not involve self-merit or works. All other religions and cults believe in a works-based system in hopes of being acceptable to their god on their own merit. God's invitation to be reconciled through belief in Jesus goes out to all people; no one, no matter what they have done, is excluded. God's desire is that all people, whether they are now agnostic or atheist, a Muslim or Buddhist, a Mormon or a Jehovah's Witness, would come to know Christ, the Savior of all mankind.

"This is good, and it is pleasing in the sight of God our Savior, who desires all people to be saved and to come to the knowledge of the truth. For there is one God, and there is one mediator between God and men, the man Christ Jesus, who gave himself as a ransom for all, which is the testimony given at the proper time" (1 Timothy 2:3-6).

Jesus said, "Come to me, all who labor and are heavy laden, and I will give you rest. Take my yoke upon you, and learn from me, for I am gentle and lowly in heart, and you will find rest for your souls" (Matthew 11:28-29).

DISCUSSION QUESTIONS:

1. Why is it critical that the Bible be authentic and historically reliable from Genesis to Revelation?

2. Why do you think that it is easy for people to accept the existence of writers such as Plato and Homer, but so passionately oppose the existence of Jesus Christ?

3. How would you respond to someone saying, "The Bible has been corrupted through the years. You just can't trust it"?

4. What is it about the way the scribes copied their manuscripts that leads you to believe that what they were writing was being copied accurately?

5. Why does it matter that there were 24,000 copies of the New Testament manuscripts?

LESSON 13 | NO FREE LUNCH

One thing many of us tend to struggle with is that Jesus' love for us is unconditional and that He has always loved us since before the beginning of time. We forget that His love never changes and that He could not have loved us more before we became a believer in Christ than after. We did absolutely nothing to deserve His love nor can we do anything to lose it. This truth about God is particularly difficult for the performer in us. We work hard in school and we get good grades, we work hard in our professions and are rewarded or we practice our skills in sports and we play better. It is easy then to see why we might conclude that if we work hard for God, we would expect to be loved more by Him. Such is not the case. When we mess up in relationships, or fail at work, or underachieve in a project, we know that we deserved the consequences and will have to work extra hard to fix what is broken. So, it would stand to reason that when we mess up in our relationship with God, He would stop loving us and break off the relationship that we had with Him—putting the burden on us to fix it. That's how we have been conditioned to think. The good news is that God is not like us. When we fail Him and ask for forgiveness, God is quick to forgive.

"If we confess our sins, he is faithful and just to forgive us our sins and to cleanse us from all unrighteousness" (1 John 1:9).

"I, even I, am he who blots out your transgressions, for my own sake, and remembers your sins no more" (Isaiah 43:25).

In the Old Testament, God demonstrated His amazing grace given to all men and women through Abraham. In Genesis 15, God tells us about the covenant, a binding agreement that God made with Abraham some 4,000 years ago, but it speaks powerfully to us today! God told Abraham that he would have many descendants that would eventually lead to the Savior. If we only consider Abraham's natural circumstances, and not God's steadfast character, we would find it hard to believe that what God was saying would actually happen. Scripture reveals Abraham's reaction:

"In hope he believed against hope, that he should become the father of many nations, as he had been told, 'So shall your offspring be.' He did not weaken in faith when he considered his own body, which was as good as dead (since he was about a hundred years old), or when he considered the barrenness of Sarah's womb. No unbelief made him waver concerning the promise of God, but he grew strong in his faith as he gave glory to God, fully convinced that God was able to do what he had promised. That is why his faith was 'counted to him as righteousness'" (Romans 4:18-22).

God also promised to give an abundance of land to Abraham and his descendants. Then came the question Abraham asked God, *"How will I know that I will possess the land? How can I know for sure that this will come to be?" (Genesis 15:8)*. God reminded Abraham that He is faithful to His word, and that He would make a binding and everlasting covenant with him that would allow Abraham to better understand what God was promising him. God then had Abraham bring to Him a three-year-old heifer, a goat and a ram along with a dove and a young pigeon. When Abraham returned with the animals, God had him split the three animals in two pieces and dig a trough between the halves to collect the blood. The birds were killed but not cut in half.

Then the covenant unfolded between God and Abraham. To paraphrase: God spoke to Abraham saying, *"I am making this covenant with you to show you how much I love you. If I fail to keep this promise concerning the land I will give to you, what happened to these animals will happen to Me."* Now it was Abraham's turn to promise the faithfulness of the people in obeying God. Abraham was filled with fear because he knew that no man could keep such a promise. God knew it too. As an act of complete unconditional love, God told Abraham that He, Himself, would step in on his behalf, by saying in essence that what has happened to the animals would happen to God if man were disobedient. Next, He put Abraham into a deep sleep. Then a smoking fire pot and a flaming torch, both representing God, passed between the animal pieces, solidifying the covenant. We all know the end of the story, nearly 2000 years later, Jesus Christ, God Himself, willingly was beaten, His body shredded (as were the bodies of the animals), died on the cross to pay the ultimate price for mankind's sin. (See Genesis 15-17, Galatians 3, Hebrews 11)

We, as humans, cannot fully understand such love and grace. God required Abraham to do nothing but believe. God did it all; proving once and for all time that we are saved by God's grace, period. All He requires of us is what He required of Abraham: to believe.

> *"Just as Abraham believed God, and it was counted to him as righteousness...so that in Christ Jesus the blessings of Abraham might come to the gentiles so that we might receive the promised Spirit through faith" (Galatians 3:6, 14).*

> *"This is how we know what love is: Jesus Christ laid down his life for us" (John 15:13).*

DISCUSSION QUESTIONS:

1. Has this lesson on the covenants between God and Abraham and between God and us opened your eyes to God's love for you in a new way?

2. What part of the covenant-making process made the deepest impression on you? Why?

3. What did it cost God to walk the road to the cross on behalf of all of us?

4. What is the significance of Abraham being in a deep sleep while the smoking fire pot and blazing torch passed between the halves of the sacrifices?

5. How does a better understanding of God's grace change your need to perform for Him?

LESSON 14 | FORWARDING ADDRESS

I don't feel renewed today. But as a Christian, shouldn't I? I was told that when I believed in Jesus, I would become a "new creation" in Christ. Shouldn't there be some inward or outward sign of the new me? Why don't I feel the love and peace that others do? My feelings are leading me back into my old insecure self. What's wrong with me?

If this is how you feel or have felt, you are in good company. Most of us have never been told that we, as believers, all go through a lifelong process (sanctification) of learning more about who God is and who we are as His children. The closer we get to God, the better we will understand what it really means to be a new creation in Christ.

> *"Therefore, if anyone is in Christ, he is a new creation. The old has passed away; behold, the new has come. All this is from God..." (2 Corinthians 5:17-18).*

Being a new creation means that we don't have to be ashamed of who we once were. We have been redeemed through the death and resurrection of Christ and are no longer guilty in the eyes of God. The shame that once covered us is gone. We are free to be all that God created us to be because of His grace! Of course we still sin, but the penalty for that sin, was paid for on the cross. The whole performance trap that used to control us, was crushed under the weight of God's great gift—making us a new creature who is loved and accepted with no hooks attached. This is the simple but profound truth! Praise God!

That is one moment...the next might be met with a thought that says, "I am not the new creation the Scriptures say I am. God cannot be trusted." Once again, such thoughts throw me into the questioning cycle that leads me back to doubt. These rollercoasters of emotions are exhausting. My fear of failure begins to increase and my desire to be transparent wanes. I revert to my old self, desiring to be accepted by others rather than simply trusting that I am always loved and accepted as God's child.

> *"So we do not lose heart. Though our outer self is wasting away, our inner self is being renewed day by day" (2 Corinthians 4:16).*

As we begin to think of the impact the cross has on each of our lives, it is important to know what God's expectations are for us. God has commanded us to love Him, to obey Him and to love others in amazing ways. He has, through His covenant love, truly made us one of His! The following is a list of some of the descriptions in the New Testament that illustrate who we are as Christ followers:

- I am the salt of the earth (Matthew 5:13).

- I am the light of the world (Matthew 5:14).

- I am a child of God (John 1:12).

- I am part of the true vine, a channel of Christ's life (John 15:1, 5).

- I am Christ's friend (John 15:15).

- I am chosen and appointed by Christ to bear His fruit (John 15:16).

- I am a new creation (2 Corinthians 5:17).

Learning to adjust to my new nature is not about "getting over it, "snapping out of it" or "just becoming humble like the rest of us." Getting to know the new me takes time and will become a reality the more time we spend reading and praying through the Scriptures. It is easy to look at others and see them as God sees them: created in the image of God, a new creation, dearly loved, designed with the purpose of loving God and others and intended to have a wonderful relationship with God. That is a biblical worldview. However, when it comes to looking in the mirror at ourselves and seeing ourselves as created in the image of God, a new creation, dearly loved, designed with purpose by a God who loves to spend time with us... now that is a different story. What is keeping us from accepting ourselves for who we really are?

Asking this question early on in our doubting moments can save a lot of heartache. If our perception of who we are in God's eyes does not match what the Bible says about us, then somewhere along the line we have bitten the apple, and ingested another one of Satan's lies. As a new creation, we can automatically dismiss a voice telling us that we are not redeemed, not forgiven, not loved by the Most High God and that we are not a new creation. The plain and overwhelmingly powerful reality is that Christ's sacrifice was enough. There is no debate about whether we are loved and redeemed by God. On the cross before He died He announced, "It is finished!" The payment was complete. It cost Christ His life, but it gave us ours.

Scripture says, *"Choose this day whom you will serve" (Joshua 24:15)*. Living out our faith does not mean we love and follow God because we feel like it. It is a choice. First, we make an intentional decision to be with Him. We pray, read the Scriptures and then ask Him to guide and direct our day so that He and He alone will get the glory. The Holy Spirit is faithful to do this! *"Now faith is being sure of what we hope for and certain of what we do not see" (Hebrews 11:1)*.

Does this new identity come with an easy life? On the contrary, this new identity will not change our circumstances, but it will revolutionize the way that we live, love, process, and react to every situation. Because God is who He says He is and we are who God says we are, our very lives become one of the ways God displays His infinite love and glory to others, whether in times of great joy or great suffering and everything in between.

DISCUSSION QUESTIONS:

1. What does it mean to be a new creation in Christ?

2. Do you find it amazing that God chooses to forget your forgiven sin?

3. How has knowing how God really looks at you changed the way you think and the way you live?

4. How can feelings mislead you about who and whose you are?

5. How might you begin your day with your focus on who God says you are?

LESSON 15 | A BEAUTIFUL LIE

One of the greatest fears for Christians, besides speaking in public, is what happens when someone asks us a question about our faith that we cannot answer? What should we do when someone verbally attacks what we believe? What can we do to defend our faith as we strive to be a light to the lost?

There are many who ask questions about Christianity because they are truly seeking answers to life's issues. Most people in this category will say they feel empty, and their life has lost meaning and direction. They know that they need something beyond themselves. These people might ask questions like: "How do you know that Jesus is the Messiah? Give me one reason to believe that the Bible is true? I'm a good person, isn't that enough to get me into heaven? How will my life be changed by believing in Jesus?" Hopefully, by now we can answer many of these questions with what we have learned from studying the previous lessons!

On the other hand, there are many who are not asking questions to learn, but rather to prove us wrong. Their goal is to attack us personally because of what we believe to be true about God and His Son, Jesus. It is critical that we know how to respond to such people when our faith comes under fire. The first thing we can do in these situations is pray and ask God to give us wisdom to speak to the soul of the one who is attacking. The idea here is not to win an argument, but to encourage the person to consider taking a second look at Christianity and their misguided presuppositions concerning Jesus. Attacking statements might include comments like: "Anyone with any brains would not believe there is a God. Only misguided people think that there is a God. Who needs a God anyway? All Christians are intolerant and judgmental. Christianity is the reason why this world is such a mess!"

How might we respond when someone makes a sweeping statement like: "There is no God!" Our response might be to ask that person: "How much of all of the knowledge and truth that has ever been made available to mankind from the beginning of time to today do you know? Is it more than 1 percent?" Accept whatever they say. Our response to their answer could be: "Might there be some truth, events and people that go beyond your own knowledge and experiences? Could there be a God, beyond your own understanding, who created and loves you and wants to give you the peace and joy in this life of which we are all looking.? I am not asking you to believe this, but rather to consider it as a possibility. Could it be true?" This opens the door to plant a seed in their mind that may cause them to question their belief that there is no God. Hopefully, result in future conversations and mentoring opportunities that will eventually lead to an understanding of the God of the Scriptures who loves unconditionally and offers peace and hope in our lives.

The Four Deadly Questions are effective questions to ask when our ideas are being attacked and we want to bring the attacker to the end of the argument. We all have opinions and convictions that are not grounded in truth, but rather in theories that we have hung on to because it was told to us by someone we love or respect. It may be something that sounds right, but upon further investigation, it is found not to be true. Such statements might include: "There is no hope in this world. Christianity is a figment of someone's imagination. God is vengeful and out to destroy. The Bible is fiction."

Our response, with love and respect, could lead the conversation through the following questions:

1.   What do you mean by that? Many brash claims lie in a weak definition of terms.

2.   How do you know that it is true? It's common for most people to have no evidence for why they believe something so strongly. This is where you can talk about how what you know to be true is found in the Scriptures. Show that person what the Bible says specifically. If they ask you how you know it is true, you can share some of the truth you have learned in the previous lessons.

3.   Where do you get your information? Be prepared to follow this up with detailed questions about how they know what they know. Before long, you will be on equal footing.

4.   What happens if you are wrong? It is one thing to claim a belief and another to stake your life and eternity on it. The most important questions to ask here are, "Where are you going when you die?" and "What happens if you are wrong?" Rarely will you ever make it to that fourth question.

The Mormons study what they believe and wear out shoe leather to bring converts into their church—and it has paid off in record numbers. The Jehovah's Witnesses do the same. The Muslims are willing to die for what they believe. Millions of cult members and those who worship false gods study their religion and are obedient to what their religion asks of them. They are passionate about living out their faith. Where are all the Christians who are students of the Scriptures and passionate about bringing others to faith in Jesus? The answer is fewer than 1 in 100. Here is the irony: the Christian religion is the only religion that is verifiable and transformational. It is true. People who live under your roof, work in your office and those you have yet to meet are starving for what you now know. God has equipped you to go into a broken and dark world. Are you willing?

> "but in your hearts honor Christ the Lord as holy, always being prepared to make a defense to anyone who asks you for a reason for the hope that is in you; yet do it with gentleness and respect..." (1Peter 3:15)

The greatest apologetic that we have is the way we live our lives. Leading with love is much more powerful than being able to answer tough questions or win an argument. When a question is asked that you don't know then tell them, "That is an excellent question. I will research it and get back with you." You might be the first person in their life to actually dialog with them about what they believe to be true. Let them know you care about them and their questions and be available to follow up with them. Some, however, might become defensive and not want to talk, which is fine. Respect their opinion and do not push them. At least you have planted a thought!

DISCUSSION QUESTIONS:

1. What questions have you been asked that have been difficult to answer?

2. Do you think that most people who believe ideas that are contrary to the Bible have done their research to support those ideas?

3. Role-play by asking someone who plays the role of a skeptic how much of all knowledge do they know.

4. Role-play with the Four Deadly Questions by starting with the statement, "There is no God!"

5. Whose voice is speaking in your head, telling you that you are not ready to talk about your faith to those who are seeking the truth?

LESSON 16 | CHARADES

In the Hebrew culture, a name was extremely important. It revealed a trait about a person, their character or a hope for their future. In the Scriptures there are 144 Hebrew names for God, with each one defining His character. God changed the names of some of His followers to better describe their new identity. God also revealed Satan's character through the many names that we find in the Scriptures. Satan is the antithesis of the character of God. Like God, Satan is always true to what his names imply. He cannot ever be any less than how he is described. Satan lives out all of these attributes in his in pursuit to destroy the hearts and minds of God's children and to distort the truth of God for those seeking to know Him.

The war that Satan is waging is not to be taken lightly. Pretending that he does not exist or that he does not have the power to make anyone's life miserable, is a big mistake. Knowing how he works, speaks, attacks and can be defeated are critical for growth in our faith. His goal is to derail our belief by devising ways to shift our focus away from God. Needless to say, he has successfully deceived millions about the truth of who God is and the eternal hope that is offered to all who believe in Jesus.

Satan (or Lucifer as he was named by God before he came to earth), was created in heaven as the guardian cherub angel. He was full of wisdom and perfect in beauty until unrighteousness was found in him (Ezekiel 28:15). He became proud because of his beauty and corrupted his wisdom by wanting to be worshiped as God. God threw him out of heaven to earth, where he continues to wreak havoc. In the end, God will destroy Satan.

Some of the names of Satan are:

1. **Tempter.**

   "And Jesus, full of the Holy Spirit, returned from the Jordan and was led by the Spirit in the wilderness for forty days, being tempted by the devil. And he ate nothing during those days. And when they were ended, he was hungry. The devil said to him, 'If you are the Son of God, command this stone to become bread.' And Jesus answered him, 'It is written, 'Man shall not live by bread alone...'" (Luke 4:1-4).

2. **Destroyer.**

   "The thief comes only to steal and kill and destroy. I came that they may have life and have it abundantly." (John 10:10); "They have as king over them the angel of the bottomless pit. His name in Hebrew is Abaddon, and in Greek he is called Apollyon" (Revelation 9:11).

3. **Accuser.**

   "And I heard a loud voice in heaven, saying, 'Now the salvation and the power and the kingdom of our God and the authority of his Christ have come, for the accuser of our brothers has been thrown down, who accuses them day and night before our God" (Revelation 12:10).

4. **Liar and murderer.**

   "You are of your father the devil, and your will is to do your father's desires. He was a murderer from the beginning, and does not stand in the truth, because there is no truth in him. When he lies, he speaks out of his own character, for he is a liar and the father of lies" (John 8:44).

5. **Blinder of minds.**

   "In their case the god of this world has blinded the minds of the unbelievers, to keep them from seeing the light of the gospel of the glory of Christ, who is the image of God" (2 Corinthians 4:4).

6. **Serpent.**

   "And the great dragon was thrown down, that ancient serpent, who is called the devil and Satan, the deceiver of the whole world—he was thrown down to the earth, and his angels were thrown down with him" (Revelation 12:9).

Satan's sole purpose is to stop us from worshiping and following God. From the looks of things, Satan and his demons are doing a great job of it. As we look at the world today, we see the continued fallout of turning away from God. Satan used his pride, greed, deceit and craftiness to cause the fall from grace in the Garden of Eden, which is still the root of the chaos that reigns throughout the world today. Every single cult promises that you can become a "god" and choose your own value and moral system. All of this goes against the very heart of God and undoubtedly grieves Him to see so many being lured into Satan's trap. The death and resurrection of Jesus paid the price for the forgiveness of all sin and gave us the power of the Holy Spirit to keep from being under Satan's control. Christ reigns victorious over Satan and his demons both now and forever!

DISCUSSION QUESTIONS:

1. Do you believe that Satan is dark energy or is he a fallen angel?

2. How does Scripture define Satan?

3. What is Satan's goal in the life of a Christian?

4. Why did Satan fall from God's grace?

5. What act of Jesus took away Satan's power in our lives?

LESSON 17 | THE KILLING FIELD

Satan is especially effective in the lives of those who deny his existence or those who are obsessed with him and blame anything that goes wrong on him. He is evil to the core and is out to kill and destroy. When people open themselves up to satanic things, anything can happen.

Satan attempts to deceive our minds by causing us to believe lies about God and lies about ourselves.. Have you ever heard these lies in your mind?

The Lie:

"You deserve to suffer. God is paying you back for all the bad things that you have done. He is so disappointed in you. There is no hope for you."

The Truth:

"Not only that, but we rejoice in our sufferings, knowing that suffering produces endurance, and endurance produces character, and character produces hope, and hope does not put us to shame, because God's love has been poured into our hearts through the Holy Spirit who has been given to us" (Romans 5:3-5).

The Lie:

"Don't worry about that lie you just told because, in the end, it makes no difference—plus it saved you from having to face someone's anger."

The Truth:

"Do not lie to one another, seeing that you have put off the old self with its practices and have put on the new self, which is being renewed in knowledge after the image of its creator" (Colossians 3:9-10).

The Lie:

"There is no hope for you. Forget it. God loves everyone else more than you."

The Truth:

"For I am sure that neither death nor life, nor angels nor rulers, nor things present nor things to come, nor powers, nor height nor depth, nor anything else in all creation, will be able to separate us from the love of God in Christ Jesus our Lord" (Romans 8:38-39).

The Lie:

"I know you have said that you put your trust in Jesus, but if you were to die right now, you would go to hell. You know that you are not really a Christian."

The Truth:

"For God so loved the world, that he gave his only Son, that whoever believes should not perish but have everlasting life" (John 3:16).

His voice. Satan does not speak to us in a foreign tongue. He speaks to us through our minds, using our own inner voice and our own vocabulary. His messages are subtle but piercing. So how can we best learn to distinguish between the voice of God and the voice of Satan? The more time we spend in the Scriptures and in prayer, the more we will be able to recognize the voice of God. Period. There is no substitute for spending time with God. And by the way, that voice that just told you that you don't have time to read and pray... that's not the voice of God!

His attack. Satan will always attack your character, because his goal is to destroy and discourage you. God will never attack your character. Instead, He will convict you of your sin, because His goal is to call you to confess so that you can be redeemed. Keep in mind that Satan can use misguided pastors, friends, spouses, children, teachers, enemies and others to do his dirty work. Satan's message might sound something like this:

"You are such a loser."

"You are worthless and no one cares for you."

"Whatever you do will fail. You are so stupid."

God might also use others to speak to you, but most importantly, He will speak and confirm what He is saying through the Holy Spirit. God's voice in convicting you of sin might sound like this:

"What you just said to her was not of Me. You need to go to her and apologize."

"The reason you are frustrated is because you are not listening to Me."

"I love you and I want you to know that there is reason for your suffering. Be a light to others, because I want to use this opportunity to bless you and others."

We are not the only ones who have been the recipients of Satan's attacks. Satan also tempted Jesus (Matthew 4:1-11 and Luke 4:1-13). How did Jesus respond?

"Jesus answered him, "It is also written: 'Do not put the Lord your God to the test. Again, the devil took him to a very high mountain and showed him all the kingdoms of the world and their splendor. "All this

I will give you," he said, *"if you will bow down and worship me." Jesus said to him, "Away from me, Satan! For it is written: 'Worship the Lord your God, and serve him only'"* (Matthew 4:7-10).

God's solution to Satan's attacks:

1. Quote Scripture. *"You, dear children are from God and have overcome them, because the one who is in you is greater than the one who is in the world" (1 John 4:4).*

2. Command Satan, in the name of Jesus and by the power of the Holy Spirit, to leave. *"Submit yourselves, then, to God. Resist the devil and he will flee from you" (James 4:7).*

How can we have victory in this life? He answered:

"'Love the Lord your God with all your heart and with all your soul and with all your strength and with all your mind'; and, 'Love your neighbor as yourself'" (Matthew 22:37, 39).

DISCUSSION QUESTIONS:

1. Do you believe that Satan is real and active in the world today? Why or why not?

2. How do you think that Satan can be most effective in derailing our faith?

3. How can you distinguish between the voice of Satan and the voice of God?

4. What has Satan told you that you now know is a lie?

5. How can you best defend yourself against his attacks?

LESSON 18 | IDENTITY THEFT

Our culture today primarily reflects the Postmodern worldview. Those who embrace Postmodernism disregard the notion of absolute truth, especially when it involves religion. "Truth is what you make it," they say. Because of this, millions of people around the world are falling into cults (counterfeit Christian religions) at an alarming rate. The Bible is filled with warnings about false teachers and leaders.

Jesus warned His apostles this would happen:

> "Then many false prophets will rise up and deceive many. And because lawlessness will abound, the love of many will grow cold" (Matthew 24:11-12).

> "Beware of false prophets, who come to you in sheep's clothing, but inwardly they are ravenous wolves" (Matthew 7:15).

From a Christian perspective, a cult is a group of people centered on the false teachings of a leader who claims that he/she is uniquely called of God. People that are pulled into cults are not bad, stupid or mean. In general, they are nice, kind, friendly and seemingly contented men and women who are following a leader who, on the outside, appears loving and kind, but on the inside is led by a heart that is deceitfully wicked.

> "For such people are false apostles, deceitful workers, masquerading as apostles of Christ. And no wonder, for Satan himself masquerades as an angel of light. It is not surprising, then, if his servants also masquerade as servants of righteousness. Their end will be what their actions deserve" (2 Corinthians 11:13-15).

A cult has a strong leader who believes he/she is supernaturally called to lead people to a new or mysterious experience. They believe that the translations of the Bible are incorrect, so they use their own translation and adopt outside books that they believe supersede the truth of the Bible. They also believe that they are the "one true church" and all others are corrupt. For them, Jesus is not God and salvation comes from good works. The beliefs of these false religions change with new revelations that may come from their leader. A cult will take a person's money, family and for many, their mind.

How does Christianity differ from a cult? Theologically, cults and Christianity have nothing in common. Our vocabularies are similar but the definitions have no resemblance to each other. Christianity says there is one God, and He is the God found in the Bible. The biblical God is one being but three separate persons: God the Father, God the Son and God the Holy Spirit. Salvation comes from God's grace when we believe in Jesus as our Savior. Salvation does not come from trying to do good things to earn God's acceptance. The Bible is our only source of authority.

An example of a counterfeit Christian religion is Mormonism. Joseph Smith, Jr. founded Mormonism in 1827. At the young age of 14, Smith said an angel named Moroni visited him and gave him golden plates with writing on them. These plates, the Mormons claim, were written in "Reformed Egyptian," a language that has never been known or heard of in all of history. By miraculous means and with special "stones set in bows" found with the plates, he was allegedly able to translate the plates into English. No one has ever seen the golden plates, which leaves their authenticity to the word of one man. The result was the Book of Mormon, published in1830. Smith also established the Mormon Church that year, calling it the "only true church."

Words matter. Thousands of cults are actively recruiting Christians and non-Christians alike into their ranks. It is vitally important to ask for a definition of terms when talking with a Mormon about his or her beliefs. The words that Christians use will be the same ones that Mormons use; however, the meanings behind the words are decidedly different. It is critical that we learn to ask the right questions to expose the lies of all false religions.

The first question to ask when inquiring about the validity of any religion is, "What do you mean ....?" To the Mormon, ask, "What do you mean when you say, 'God is my Father in heaven?'" If they answer according to their own writings, they would say that God is a 6-foot-tall, physical "exalted man." His name is "Elohim." Once only a mere human, he had to learn to become god. He has a father, and there are many gods above him. He is only the "god of this universe."[14] Ask a Mormon what they mean when they talk about Jesus Christ being God's Son. The answer is that they believe Jesus Christ was a spirit baby born to the Heavenly Father and one of his goddess wives, "Heavenly Mother." They named him "Jehovah." God is married to many women and cannot create anything from nothing. He had sex with his wife to produce Jesus pre-mortally, as well as all of humanity by the same method. Lucifer, the Devil, is also one of Jesus' "spiritual brothers."[15] These are just a few examples of Mormon beliefs that distort the truth of God and Scripture.

So, based on the Mormon definitions and the history of this religion, is Mormonism a cult? Yes, it is. It is not because these people are evil—quite the contrary. These people have been misled to think that by joining forces, following rules and an earthly leader, they will find fulfillment in this life. Only the person of Jesus Christ of the Bible can give us life and give it to us abundantly. Our responsibility as Christians is not to sit back and judge, but to live out our faith in Jesus by loving Mormons as friends and being ready to give them the reason for the hope that we have in Jesus and His grace with gentleness and respect.

DISCUSSION QUESTIONS:

1. Could you be one who would walk away from your Christian faith? Why?

2. When being invited to join a religious group, why is it important to ask, "Who do you say Jesus is?"

3. Compare the Mormon meaning of "God the Father" to the Christian meaning.

4. Is it judgmental to believe that Mormonism is a cult? Why or why not?

5. Why is it so important to have a strong understanding of the Christian faith?

LESSON 19 | THE GAMBLE

Depending on who you talk to, some might think that we can become Christians by repeating a prayer, being baptized or joining a church. Attending services at least 90 percent of the time, putting 10 percent of our income into the offering plate, praying out loud, participating in a mission trip, singing in the choir or actively and cheerfully serving on a least one church committee might also be requirements. The truth is, becoming a Christian is not about any of these things. Period.

As we saw in a previous lesson, Abraham believed God and it was credited to him as righteousness. John 3:16 states, *"whoever believes in him (Christ) will not perish but have eternal life."* Notice how this passage does not say, "whoever joins a committee or whoever repeats this prayer will have eternal life." The Greek word for believe, pisteuo, means "to be persuaded of or to place confidence in, to trust". As conditioned performers, our natural response might be, "Yes, I know I should believe in Him, but what do I have to do to become a Christian? How do I prove I am a Christian? I have to do something to feel like I have contributed, even in just some little way." While we may think these things, God knows our hearts and sees our belief in Him and that is what matters. Remember, Abraham simply believed God, and that is all God is asking us to do: to believe in His one and only Son, Jesus Christ, who died for our sins and rose again. This truth is profoundly simple, but the impact is transformational.

There is confusion in the minds of many people who have made different claims of faith. I think all of us fall into one of the following categories of people of faith:

Group one are those who are saved by faith through Christ and know it. They are those who believe that Jesus Christ is God and died for their sins and rose again. They have assurance that they are God's children, that the Bible is true and that when they die they will go to heaven. They are lights who shine God's love and grace to others.

Group two includes those who are saved by faith through Christ and do not know it. They think that there must be something more that they must do in order to become one of His children. They do not understand grace. Others in this group have been so beaten down by those around them that they believe the lie that says they are unworthy of God's grace. They simply do not know what to do with God's love.

Group three are those who are not saved by faith through Christ and know it. These are individuals who have heard the truth of Christ and have knowingly rejected it. Many fear that they would have to commit intellectual suicide to become a Christian and trust in Christ. They want to be in control of their own lives and therefore have no choice but to reject the belief of Jesus as their Lord and Savior.

Group four are those who are not saved by faith through Christ and do not know it. They think they are Christians, but are not. Many of these people are so performance minded that they believe being a Christian only involves going to church and following the rules. Many were raised in Christian homes and did what was expected of them, but never developed an authentic relationship with Him.. They know how to speak Christianese, but their hearts are set on their own agenda. The hypocrites hide out in this group. They might attend Bible studies and go to church because it is the thing to do, but inwardly their hearts are set on worldly things. They live in a world of duplicity: being "religious" has little if any effect on how they live out their lives.

Matthew 7:16-20 says,

> *"By their fruit you will recognize them. Do people pick grapes from thorn bushes, or figs from thistles? Likewise every good tree bears good fruit, but a bad tree bears bad fruit. A good tree cannot bear bad fruit, and a bad tree cannot bear good fruit. Every tree that does not bear good fruit is cut down and thrown into the fire. Thus, by their fruit you will recognize them."*

If God is convicting you through the Holy Spirit, that you are one of the people in the fourth group, know that God is a God of second chances. He is calling you to an authentic faith in Him. He is asking you to come clean with Him and confess the emptiness of your heart and ask Him to cleanse you of all unrighteousness. There is nothing that you have done or that you have failed to do that God will not forgive.

We Must Make a Choice

Maybe it is time, right now, to stop and honestly consider where you are with Christ the Lord. If Christ is who He says He is, then the question is, "Who do you say He is?" Are you giving Him an intellectual nod of existence, or are you trusting Him with your life? As with any new relationship, it takes time to know someone intimately—so it is with God. It does not mean that you have to love Him immediately; that will come in time. All He is asking is that you believe that He died for all of your sins: past, present and future. He rose again, proving to you, and to the world, that He lives and you will be with Him forever. That, my friend, is the Gospel, the great news!

Because the Holy Spirit lives in believers, we can, through Him, be *"the light of the world" (Matthew 5:14).* Further down in verse 16, He says, *"…let your light shine before others, so that they may see your good works and give glory to your Father who is in heaven."* We live as lights so others can see Jesus through us and understand what it means to follow Him as we love God and love others.

DISCUSSION QUESTIONS:

1. Why is the message of salvation so difficult for some people to believe?

2. What does it mean to believe in Jesus?

3. Who is the Holy Spirit? Is He any less than Jesus or the Father?

4. Can we believe in Jesus as our Savior, but not have the Holy Spirit living in us?

5. How do you know that God will never leave you?

DISCUSSION QUESTIONS:

1. Why is the message of salvation so difficult for some people to believe?

2. What does it mean to believe in Jesus?

3. Who is the Holy Spirit? Is He any less than Jesus or the Father?

4. Can we believe in Jesus as our Savior, but not have the Holy Spirit living in us?

5. How do you know that God will never leave you?

LESSON 20 | NOW WHAT?

Why is it that some people just get it? You know, they are the ones who are clearly… living out their faith in Christ and thriving, no matter the circumstances. They are far from perfect and know it but they love the Lord. They have a passion to learn, pray, listen, serve God, and to be a light by mentoring others along the way. They freely share about their faith and have a desire to interact with others who are searching for answers about God, life and death.

Mixed among them are Christians, who are nice people, but have little passion for Christ. Their conversations and life generally do not reflect Christ. Many put in their time by attending church and giving money to worthy organizations, but that is about it. Their desire to learn more about the Christian faith and about God is minimal. The thought of praying is something they do not do because, frankly, they do not know how. Most of these people are the way they are because they have not been taught how to have a strong faith that is life changing. The good news is that they do not have to stay this way.

Getting to know God is like any other healthy relationship: the more time you spend together and the more you learn about Him, the more you will grow to trust and love Him. Spending time with God on a daily basis helps us begin to see how much He is involved in our lives. With God at work in us, we will gain insight into people and problems that we have not had before. When difficult situations come up, the peace we have knowing God is in us and will walk with us through everything makes things so much easier. When we choose to spend time getting to know Him, He changes the desires of our hearts; He teaches us truth and conforms us to become more like Him so, when people see "something different" about us, they see Jesus living in us!

There is no exact formula for growing close to God. We are all uniquely different and express ourselves in our own way. We worship God through prayer, reading and meditating on the Scriptures. It is through these disciplines, that our hearts are opened to receive His truth, love and plan for our lives. There are no shortcuts.

"And I am sure of this, that he who began a good work in you will bring it to completion at the day of Jesus Christ" (Philippians 1:6).

For most all of us, the concept of prayer is extremely difficult and mysterious. Many wonder if God cares enough to listen to them because so few of their prayers are answered. Does prayer really matter and does it make a difference? Why does God seem so distant at times? Why do I feel like I am the only one who doesn't get my prayers answered?

When we pray and for how long is not the issue; making time with God a top priority in our life is the issue. We show our love for God by reading His Word.

We worship God in our own way by thanking Him for who He is and for who we are because of Him.

Prayer is talking with God, not in the King James English, but in our own way of speaking.

God wants to know what is on our heart and He wants us to know what is on His. He desires that we understand how much He loves us and thinks about us. He loves for us to come to Him as we are, especially when we are weak and spiritually filthy. He wants us to be brutally honest with Him about our struggles and our sin. Knowing that He died for our sins, we can boldly ask Him to forgive us for whatever He is prompting us to say—don't forget to thank Him and forgetting sin! *"For I will be merciful toward their iniquities, and I will remember their sins no more" (Hebrews 8:12).*

Following Christ through the reading of Scripture is the heartbeat of this study. God has not called us to check off a list of dos and don'ts or keep track of all the good we have done. What He wants is for us to worship Him as we live our lives. No one has said it is easy—it is not. However, the joy that we have in living with Christ goes beyond human expression. Jesus' instructions are short and to the point and will not only change us, but our world as well!

> *"And behold, a lawyer stood up to put him to the test, saying, 'Teacher, what shall I do to inherit eternal life?' He said to him, 'What is written in the Law? How do you read it?' And he answered, 'You shall love the Lord your God with all your heart and with all your soul and with all your strength and with all your mind, and your neighbor as yourself.' And he said to him, 'You have answered correctly; do this, and you will live" (Luke 10:25-28).*

DISCUSSION QUESTIONS

1. Why do you think some people live out their faith while others don't?

2. Why is it critical to spend time with God beyond a Sunday sermon?

3. What would you say to someone who says that God does not answer prayer?

4. How important is it to God that you have a relationship with Him?

5. Can you say that it is a privilege to obey God? Why or why not?

LESSON 21 | MOVE AHEAD

Two of our sons learned to ski the same day. The instructor took them up the mountain and gave them the basic instructions necessary for them to get moving on the snow. He taught them how to snowplow and assured them that when they had some more practice, they could ski down the steeper slopes. Then, the instructor told them to follow him and off they went slowly down the hill one behind the other. One son followed, but the other one soon decided that he wanted to speed things up, so he turned his skis toward the bottom of the hill and took off. Things quickly got out of control and he took a hard fall. By the grace of God, he avoided sliding into several trees and eventually came to a halt halfway down the slope.. His skis and poles were strewn over the slope, looking a bit like a garage sale. He suffered a few bruises but, now a bit wiser, was given a second chance to ski. This time he was ready to follow his leader!

It has been our desire that you have, over the past several weeks, learned more about the foundations of the Christian faith and have a better understanding of who God is and how much He loves you. Unless you have a firm foundation with some solid instruction for living out your faith, you too will have many collisions and bruises along your journey.

One of the most difficult disciplines of being a Christian is to learn to be content in Christ alone. Because of our propensity to perform, many of us make the mistake of thinking that we must join Bible studies, get on committees and attend multiple Christian functions. The end result of following what looks like a good thing to do is often busyness that will eventually shout over the voice of God. Before long, our Christian life will turn into activities, rather than a meaningful relationship with Christ. It is in the quiet times with God that we get our direction, our knowledge of truth and our passion for loving God and others that transcends our own understanding. Over time, we hear the voice of God telling us to: be a reflection of Him in all areas of life, to be ready to engage with people and to love them right where they are by getting to know them, and to give the reason for the hope that we have in Jesus.

If our friends and co-workers are seeking God either knowingly or unknowingly, where are they going to find Him? If they are not going to a well-grounded church and don't hang around with Christian friends, then where are they going to find answers? Christ does not drop us off at work and wait for us until we get home. He is in us all the time! That is why God designed us in His image so that, through us, people could learn about Jesus simply by watching us. Hopefully others will see Christ's love, encouragement, hope and integrity lived out through us.

If we are not students of our faith, we will be ineffective communicators of what it means to be a Christian and how one can live Christ out in all of life. Understanding what we believe and how we can know it is truth is important not just for our own affirmation, but for sharing it with others as well. Having a good grasp of what other religions embrace is hugely important because it enables us to intelligently discuss issues with others of different faiths. Through rational discourse, we can teach and challenge others without getting defensive and speaking about things of which we have little or no knowledge. Admitting we have no clue how to answer some questions can be a good thing. It is refreshing to actually have a discourse with a Christian who admittedly does not have all the answers, but will try to find them!

We worship an awesome God. In love He created us, but we chose to go our own way. He pursued us, forgave us and then we went our own way again. He promised He would send the Messiah to pay the price for our sins. Mankind continued to sin and were fickle in their faith, but God's faithfulness never wavered. He came to earth in human form and showed us how to live, to love and to die. He fulfilled His promise of sending a Savior by suffering and dying on a cross.

What amazes me is that after the death and resurrection of Christ, God chose to no longer reside in the temple on the Ark of the Covenant. The ark was in a separate room called the Holy of Holies with a thick curtain that separated God from the Jewish priests. The curtain was symbolic of God being separated from man because of sin. When Christ died for the sins of all men and women, the curtain in the temple that separated man from God was ripped from top to bottom. Not only did that mean that people now had direct access to God but also that God could come off of the Ark of the Covenant. He could have chosen to live anywhere. There are some beautiful churches and cathedrals and vistas throughout the world, but God did not want to live there. Instead He chose to live in those who believe in Him, that is you and me, and through us, into the world! What a privilege! Amazing Grace!

> "Do you not know that you are God's temple and that God's Spirit dwells in you? If anyone destroys God's temple, God will destroy him. For God's temple is holy, and you are that temple" (1 Corinthians 3:16-17).

> "And I heard the voice of the Lord saying, 'Whom shall I send, and who will go for us?' Then I said, 'Here I am! Send me.' And he said, 'Go...'" (Isaiah 6:8).

DISCUSSION QUESTIONS

1. What is the most valuable life giving truth that you learned from this study?

2. Why difference does it make in your life to know that God lives in you all of the time?

3. Are you learning to be still and listen to God in the midst of the busyness of your life?

4. Are you convinced that God is all you need?

5. Where is He sending you? Are you willing? Are you ready?

ENDNOTES

1. Merriam-Webster dictionary.

2. http://www.goodreads.com/author/quotes/1197.Harold_Pinter.

3. http://www.goodreads.com/author/show/73439.Taylor_Mali.

4. http://www.goodreads.com/author/show/2476.Noam_Chomsky.

5. Wells, David F. No Place for Truth: Or, Whatever Happened to Evangelical Theology. Grand Rapids: William B. Eerdmans Publishing Company, 1994.

6. Lewis, C.S. The Problem of Pain. New York: Macmillan Publishing, 1978.

7. Ibid.

8. Sir Fred Hoyle. "Hoyle on Evolution". Nature, vol. 294, 12 Nov. 1981, p. 105.

9. "Is a new and general theory of evolution emerging?" Paleobiology, vol. 6 (1), January 1980, p. 127.

10. The Weekend Australian, 7-8 May 1983, p.3.

11. McElveen, Floyd. God's Word, Final, Infallible and Forever. Grand Rapids: Gospel Truths Ministries, 1985.

12. Stoner, Peter. Science Speaks. Chicago: Moody Press, 1958. Ed. Donald W. Stoner, 2002.

13. Josephus, Flavius. The Works of Josephus. Trans. William Whiston. Peabody, MA: Hendrickson Publishers, 1987.

14. Joseph Smith, Journal of Discourses Volume 6, (Salt Lake City, UT: The Church of Jesus Christ of Latter Day Saints, 1844), p. 3-5.

15. Joseph Smith, Journal of Discourses Volume 6, (1844), p. 8. Also see: Brigham Young, Journal of Discourses, Volume 8 (1860), p. 268.

APPENDIX

Your Turn

Thank you for traveling on this journey with us. Our deepest desire is that you will start or continue living a culture changing life with a Christian worldview as your compass. Our hope is that your life will reflect what Christ has done, and is doing in you each and every day. We challenge you to always be ready to share the truth of Christ and the life that He offers, to anyone who asks.

Now that you have gone through the *Unanswered: Smoke, Mirrors, and God* study, you are in a great position to take what you have learned and teach juniors and seniors in high school with the Anchorsaway Christian worldview curriculum. This curriculum is designed to be taught by adults as a community study in a home setting. It is for anyone who is either questioning their faith or wants to deepen their faith with solid answers from history, science, the Bible and scholars who are experts in their respective fields. Not only will Anchorsaway students learn with clarity about the hope they have, but they will also be armed to answer questions about their faith with confidence in an unbelieving world!

The curriculum covers 21 major questions that are listed below. It can be taught by a trained teacher or through videos. If you are interested, please go to our website for more information. On our site, you can learn more about who we are and even sign up for an online teacher training class. Our website is anchorsaway.org.

Chapters offered in the Anchorsaway Curriculum:

1. What is the Christian Worldview?
2. What are the Five Major Worldviews?
3. Who is God?
4. Is the Bible Reliable?
5. Was Jesus Christ Resurrected? Why Does it Matter?
6. Is Jesus Christ God? What is the Trinity?
7. What is a Christian? Am I One?
8. Did Life Just Happen or Were We Created?
9. Who is the god of Islam?
10. What is the Big Picture of God's Redemption of Man?
11. Who is Satan and How Does He Work?
12. What is a Cult?
13. Why Don't the Jews Believe in Jesus?
14. How Does God View the Homosexual?
15. What are the Moral Implications of Bioethics?
16. What is the Christian Role in Cultural Reconciliation?
17. What are the Biblical Principles to Wise Financial Planning?
18. How can I become a Leader Who Influences Culture for Christ?
19. Why Does God allow Suffering?
20. How Do I Make Good Life choices?
21. What are the Keys to Building Healthy Relationships?

NOTES

NOTES